WHEELS UP!

Second edition – published 2009

First published in 2003 by
WOODFIELD PUBLISHING LTD
Bognor Regis ~ West Sussex ~ England ~ PO21 5EL
www.woodfieldpublishing.co.uk

ISBN 1-903953-39-1

Wheels Up!

An RAF Boy Entrant's Story

BOB 'TAFF' PRICE

Woodfield

Woodfield Publishing Ltd

Woodfield House ~ Babsham Lane ~ Bognor Regis ~ West Sussex ~ PO21 5EL
telephone 01243 821234 ~ **e-mail** enquiries@woodfieldpublishing.co.uk

Interesting and informative books on a variety of subjects

For full details of all our published titles, visit our website at
www.woodfieldpublishing.co.uk

*This Book is dedicated
to all those who went through
the rigours of Boy Entrant training
no matter what their entry, trade or station*

*Welcome! - My Name is CORPORAL!
and I'm Going to be like a Mother and
Father to you for the Next 13 Weeks!*

~ CONTENTS ~

A Boy Entrant Ode

From lowly backgrounds we all came
Thought not good enough for apprentice fame
Accents strong, dressed Sunday best
We arrived to begin our determined quest.

Allegiance given, dressed in blue
Heads held high, what a motley crew
They broke us down and built us up
Whatever became of that flabby pup.

The square to bash and back to school
The room to bull, the daily rule
Short arm inspections, naked shame
Fit and healthy was the name of the game

Each week we'd wait for that special day
The point in time we'd collect our pay
Stepping forward – "SIR," we'd boom
Here's a quid, son, now leave the room!

To the NAAFI for buns and tea
Bromide laced it was said to be
Off to the Astra like a band of brothers
One cigarette shared with fourteen others

The good old Chipmunk for our first flight
The parachute straps pulled far too tight
Your turn arrives, all wish you luck
Then walk to the aircraft like a crippled duck!

Stood to attention at the end of the bed
For the kit inspections we'd come to dread
"NOT BLOODY GOOD ENOUGH," they'd scream and roar
Up in the air our kit would soar.

Marching and drill they couldn't fault
Each day we'd improve our sliding halt
"That's not in the book," the D.Is would bark
But we were brats – it was our trademark

Half way through, we're beginning to win
No longer sprogs – new entries are in
We're different from them, it's easy to tell
Tougher and fitter and riding the swell.

Berets shrunk and shaped to fit
We do look different – well, just a bit
Now senior entry, we have a ball
Trade training finished, we know it all

One week to go to our passout parade
All getting ready for the final charade
You do feel different from all the rest
You've beaten the system and passed the test

Postings through, you study the maps
Discard the chequered bands from around your caps
Kitbag shouldered, you're ready to go
Saying farewell to the friends that you know

Now we're older, reminiscing in chats
Remembering the days when we were brats
Memories fade but what the hell
We've been there - that's all we need tell

With grateful thanks to Chas (Taff) Truman (25th Air Wirless R.A.F Cosford) for giving permission to include his poignant ode in the book and for allowing me to amend it slightly to reflect my own era. B.P.

Acknowledgements

My Thanks go to all the ex-boys who helped me with my research and jogged my memory when it was needed. To Charlie Gibson, who went to such extraordinary lengths to contact everyone in the 43rd entry to arrange a re-union and for dragging me back into the fold by introducing me to the Boy Entrants Association. To the Association themselves, my thanks are extended for their permission to use certain archive information from their excellent booklet *The Formative Years*.

For his wonderful photographs of the Bren gun and Lee Enfield rifle, my gratitude goes to Toby Brayley. To Mickie Collins for his rib-tickling cartoons depicting the funny side of boy entrant life and to all the lads on the boy entrant website BEACHAT for their support and hilarious input into suggesting a title for the book (none of them were used!). To John Ward (41st Entry Teleg.) for providing part of the cover graphics (not to mention his excellent company at the last reunion). Finally, to Clive Brooks, who took several years to teach me to write proper and who guided me, with wild abandon, into a literary wilderness!

Introduction

As early as 1934, the Royal Air Force took on Boy Entrants to commence training as wireless operators, photographers and armourers. It was the beginning of a proud tradition that saw boys as young as fifteen enter into a service environment that was both rigorous and demanding.

Boy Entrant training was suspended during the war years but re-commenced in 1947 with the 1st Entry and continued through to 1965 when the 51st Entry passed out from St Athan, Cosford and Hereford. By this time, nearly every trade in the R.A.F had been included in the boy entrant training programme.

Apart from their schoolboy looks, it wasn't difficult to identify boy entrants. Chequered hatbands and the four bladed propeller 'wheel' worn on the left sleeve identified them immediately. The hatbands came in a variety of colours, denoting which station you came from. At Hereford, for example, our hatbands were red and white.

Thousands of boys went through the training period of eighteen months, a time of strict discipline and rigorous activity. Many fell by the wayside and it wasn't unusual for an entry to pass out several down on their original number of boys. Some were relegated (back-entried) to try again and some didn't even sign on, electing to take advantage of the 24 hour 'make your mind up' option. I'm quite sure that many of them are now viewing that course of action with some regret.

For all of us who went through those intense times, it didn't really register at the time that we were perhaps going through a unique period in the history of the Royal Air Force. It was only later, when we moved on to man's service, that we began to realise that we'd been through a training programme that very few had endured or even heard about. I'm sure I wasn't the only ex-boy entrant who stamped to attention (much to their consternation!) in front of a startled section corporal on the first day of our new posting from boys service.

Boys joined for different reasons. Some went, more or less, straight from school because they wanted nothing more than to join the R.A.F. Others went because they were heading down the slippery slope to a life on the dole with the possibility of drifting into a life of crime. Whatever the reason, they joined and they learned the true value of comradeship and discipline, both self and imposed. Today, many years on, there are plenty of us who freely acknowledge that those invigorating eighteen months helped shape our characters and enabled us to approach the rest of our lives with confidence and, yes, maybe just a little bit of arrogance as well!

This book is not an authoritative journal, nor do I seek to impose my own view on others. There may be inaccurate statements and incorrect information that many may leap on with outrage and self-righteous indignation and quite rightly so. My only excuse is a maturing memory!

My entry, the 43rd, commenced training in 1961 but there were boys who joined long before we did and, as we all do when 'shooting a line,' they come out with sayings like, "You think you had it tough, well back in '38, '51, 58 etc..."

This is the way of things and it's all taken in good part when we reminisce over the Internet or at our various re-unions. The fact remains that all of us, no matter when we joined, shared the experience of a lifetime - an experience that keeps many of us together to this day.

I hope that I've adequately conveyed the realities of boy entrant life in this book. The comradeship, the hardships (some real, some imagined!) and the tremendous fun of those exciting times – times that held so much promise of forthcoming adventures in foreign lands. Did we ever suffer from stress and depression? I suppose we must have (our drill instructors would have been disappointed if we hadn't!) but we weren't given the time to dwell on it too much. I sometimes feel that modern psychologists could learn a lot from corporal drill instructors!

Bob (Taff) Price

Instructor: Repeat After Me:

" If It's In Stock, You Can't Have It -
Because Somebody Else Might Need It !'"

1.   Rude Awakenings

"Am I too young to join the R.A.F?" I asked nervously, poking my head around the door of the recruiting office in Cardiff.

"How old are you, son?" the smartly dressed sergeant asked, eyeing my school uniform with some suspicion.

"Fifteen, Sergeant," I told him reluctantly.

"Step this way, young man – I've got the very thing for you," he beamed. "We call them 'Boy Entrants'."

(Later on, I learned that 'Boy Entrants' wasn't the only thing they called them, but it was obviously considered bad form to mention this prior to my 'signing on the dotted line'!)

The year was 1961, the beginning of the swinging sixties – free love, psychedelic partying and flowing hairstyles...

Sometimes, I feel quite sorry that I missed it all.

We were sent to R.A.F Cardington in Bedford for the selection interviews and I travelled up wearing my ATC (Air Training Corps) uniform, as instructed. This turned out to be a mistake, as everyone else thought I must have known what I was doing and followed my lead. When it became apparent that I was as clueless as they were, most of them sloped off in different directions.

Our first night at Cardington proved a touch traumatic for the more delicate souls in our billet – it was the first time we'd ever been shouted and sworn at with venomous intent. It followed a massive pillow fight, with lots of juvenile screaming and shouting accompanying the mayhem. The billet door had flown open and a dreadful apparition in blue filled the doorframe.

"PACK IT IN YOU BUNCH OF SURGICAL PRICKS OR I'LL COME IN THERE AND DISEMBOWEL EVERY F***ING ONE OF YOU!"

We guessed he might have been a medic!

As a showstopper, I've yet to find a better one and it quietened us down on the instant.

"*Jee-zus*, talk about over the top!" whispered a London accent, after the airman had stormed off in a high dudgeon. Then, displaying very little of the qualities required for potential steely-eyed airmen, we crept quietly into our pits and didn't as much as murmur for the rest of the night!

I'd been a bit surprised when I was asked to give three choices of trade because I hadn't given trade training a lot of thought. I don't really know what I expected from the Royal Air Force other than to be given the opportunity to fly a lot! I put MT mechanic as first choice, armourer as second and supply as third. I didn't really know what supply was but didn't think it mattered a great deal as I expected to be given my first choice anyway!

A few searching questions about engines ("Well, to be honest, sir, I've really no idea what a spark plug is!) and my potential career as a mechanic was over. My knowledge of arms boiled down to the fact that I was a pretty good shot with a .22 rifle and knew which end the bullet came out of.

"I think, with careful consideration, that you may be suited to one of the less technical trades," I was told by a weary looking flight lieutenant.

I was accepted as a supplier (the other squadrons simplified this to 'store-basher').

The arrival at Hereford railway station was chaotic. Multitudes of youthful looking civilians with strange accents milled helplessly about the platform before being herded aboard a fleet of three-ton trucks for the bumpy journey to RAF Hereford (Credenhill). This was going to be our home for the next eighteen months.

Those who didn't fall by the wayside over the coming months anyway!

*"I'll never forget arriving at Hereford railway station, suitcase in hand, looking down those steps to the start of the greatest adventure I'd ever embark on. It's still vivid in my mind and remains my most memorable recollection of those early days. I was fifteen at the time but looked about twelve!" (**Chris Boxsey** 3 Sqn)*

We were quickly sorted into our various squadrons and marched (we got a lot better at this marching business over the next year or so!) down to our allotted billets. My expectations of grandiose accommodation began to fade rapidly as we made our way down the main drag to our living quarters. All around us were large, drab looking wooden huts, very much like those seen on all the best prisoner of war films.

"Poor sods," I can remember thinking, "I wonder who has to live in THEM."

On the way down, we were passed by a gaggle of uniformed boy entrants and we experienced our first taste of 'Time-in-ism.'

"SPROGS – SUCKERS – YOU'LL BE SOORRRRYYYYY," they hollered with an indecent amount of glee and malice as we goggled at them in astonishment.

We were allotted huts 191, 192 and 193. Hut 191 was to be my home until the R.A.F decided to move us into buildings that were actually fit for human habitation.

The huts were long, wooden buildings, heated by two pot bellied, coal burning stoves. To the rear of our hut was the ablutions block, heated by absolutely nothing. During the winter months, the piece of open ground between the hut and ablutions block became a real hazard zone as scantily dressed, freezing cold boy entrants hurtled back and forth with scant regard for anybody in the way. You couldn't take any short cuts with hygiene either – the dreaded snap foot inspections took care of that (more of this heinous practice later).

The huts accommodated about sixteen boy entrants apiece.

One of the 46th entry draftees summed up the accommodation in very eloquent terms.

"My mum keeps her hens in a shed like that," he said bluntly, before catching the next bus back to civilisation.

We were given 24 hours to change our minds and remain on Civvy Street. Only one took the option. The rest of us were sworn in and presented with ten shillings to buy two locks for our wooden lockers; these and a Spartan, metal framed bed were our sole possessions as far as furniture went. We were now 'A' Flight, Number 3 Squadron, 43rd Entry of Boy Entrants, R.A.F Hereford – 'Brats' to the rest of the Royal Air Force.

It didn't take us long to get our nicknames. Whispered introductions took place after lights out on the first night and these took the form of, "Where you from, mate?"

"Cardiff," unsurprisingly, lumbered me with 'Taff' for the rest of my service life.

Paddy Jenkins represented the Emerald Isles, whilst Haggis Gibson did the honours for Scotland. Most of the others in our hut were from boring places so had to make do with their own names or names that were later to be foisted on them for one reason or another. Ken was no bother though. At well over 6ft and towering over the rest of us, he could only be known ever after as

Lofty. We went to sleep feeling a little less lonely than we had a very short while ago.

SLAAAAMMMM! The billet door flew open and a manic, shouting creature stormed through the billet in a matter of seconds.

I can't remember the exact words we were woken up with on our first morning but it wasn't, "Good morning, gentlemen – sorry to disturb you at this hour – anybody like a cup of tea?"

It was 6am, or 0600 as we'd know it from now on. It was a very bad time to be starting the day and I could see that I wasn't alone in my opinion. The shock of this awakening was horrendous, with the majority of us struggling to remember exactly where we were. One thing only registered. It was very, very unfunny!

All of us were on our feet, giving a grotesque impression of rabbits who'd just watched a snake pass through their warren! The smell of sweaty, juvenile bodies mingled with the faint aroma of creosoted wood and floor polish as we looked at each other. The unspoken question was in everyone's eyes...

"Christ! What the f**k was THAT?"

After the first communal wash, most of us attempted to bashfully dress behind our locker doors in furtive haste. It didn't take us long to lose our shyness though. We had other, rather more important matters to occupy our minds during the coming months.

Breakfast was not an option. Breakfast was compulsory and it was on that first morning that 4 Squadron (cooks and bottle washers) got their first taste of what they were training for. We queued for our breakfast and were queue-bashed by the senior entry. This was their prerogative but we didn't know it at that early stage.

"Hey! mush, the queue starts this end," someone said as he was shouldered aside. A hush seemed to fall as the queue basher turned to see who had dared to question his right. Spotting the civilian clothes, he relaxed a little and came over to the lippy one.

"Look," he said, in a reasonable sort of voice, "I'm in the senior entry, okay? You are brand, spanking new and we call you sprogs, okay? We, being the senior entry, queue bash everybody – particularly sprogs, okay?

Knowing that his reply would probably determine his immediate well-being, the lippy one agreed that this was certainly okay by him and that, had he been aware of the protocol regarding these matters, he wouldn't have dreamed of opening his mouth in the first place. It actually came out as,

"Yeah, alright – sorry, mate."

The mess hall seemed huge, with long tables filling the interior. I noticed there were no flowers, table napkins or finger bowls set out. I guessed these would be in place for the evening meal! The serving area was manned by cooks (or unfortunate souls on fatigues) stood behind each stainless steel serving dish or tray. A corporal supervisor prowled behind them.

"When I say a ladle of chips, I mean a LEVEL ladle of chips and when some silly bastard says he only likes his eggs sunny-side-up, you draw the young gentleman to my attention, right?"

Corporal cooks are a tetchy breed and when they ask if there are any complaints, it's best not to voice an opinion. On our first day, the duty corporal approached us with this very question on his lips. He was brandishing a meat cleaver at the time and, although we'd been told this was his little joke with all the new boys, nobody felt like testing the water by making a complaint.

"No, corporal," we chorused with enthusiasm.

"Excellent, excellent," he beamed, "By the way, I'll take it as a personal insult if you don't clear every scrap of food off those plates."

4 Squadron looked delighted. This seemed like the sort of life they could relate to in a big way.

Eating habits varied enormously. Some tried to retain a certain dignity with knife and fork whilst others used them like shovels! Meal times were there for restoring energy levels though and picky eaters quickly got over their aversions to certain foods. If you were hungry (16 hours out of the 24 usually – the other 8 being reserved for sleeping) anything edible would do. I had a peculiar craving for corn flakes, loads of sugar and cold milk when I went to bed hungry one night. I even dreamed about it and when morning came, I was first in the queue at breakfast. The corn flakes were Delicious.

The next little educational foray came in the form of a welcoming address by our flight lieutenant ("pronounced lef-ten-ant and don't let me hear ANYONE refer to me as the 'flight looey'").

"My name is Flight Lieutenant Gamble. You will call me 'Sir'. You will NOT call me mate, mush, pal, cocker or any other name of a similar nature."

He looked pointedly at Eddie Edwards, who'd asked him the time (in overly familiar terms) the previous day.

"These wings on my uniform indicate that I'm an aeroplane driver and sometimes I still go off and drive aeroplanes, but for now, I'm here to look after you. Are there any questions?"

"Yes, sir – when do we go on leave?" Eddie Edwards again, with a huge grin, as though this was the first time his little joke had ever been cracked in a service environment.

I could see that Eddie was being marked down as a troublemaker, and we'd only been there a day!

Naturally, we were itching to get into uniform and it wasn't long before we were marched off to stores for our standard issue of kit. We staggered out with boots, webbing, shirts, draws cellular (horrendous garments masquerading as underpants) and all the other paraphernalia, boy entrants for the use of. The shirts were collarless and we were provided with separate collars and collar studs. These little instruments of torture mercilessly branded every single boy entrant with a permanent bruise to the back and front of their scrawny necks. Breathing wasn't all that easy either, not in the first couple of weeks anyway. By that time, we'd learned how to breathe through our noses!

The standard uniform of the boy entrant prior to obtaining number 1 (dress) and number 2 (work) uniforms, was a one-piece denim overall, boots, webbing belt, shirt, tie and a beret. Berets had a mind of their own and it never ceased to amaze me how many different shapes they took on whilst adorning some grinning idiot's bonce. There was the standard 'flying saucer' shape, the 'withered mushroom' fashion or the old favourite, the 'look at me, I'm a total nerd' design.

A lesson in shaping the beret to the head proved invaluable and a lot of ripping out of linings and soaking of headgear followed. It was quite a sight to see boy entrants in all sorts of undress garb wandering around the billet with sopping wet berets bonding nicely to their aching heads.

We were beginning to pick up a few tricks of the trade.

Sergeant Thomas and Corporal Tommy Temple made themselves known to us at the outset and it was to these two ramrod straight NCOs that we were to owe so much at the end of our training. Tommy Temple was RAF Regiment ("It's the army, son") and he was a hard, tough man who dragged us through our eighteen months with no regard whatsoever for any finer feelings we may have felt we were entitled to. We swore about him a lot but we were proud of him as well and we were proud of ourselves at the end, thanks largely to his unrelenting efforts. .

Sergeant Thomas was an immaculate man with a wonderful voice that could carry for miles and a pace stick that could pinpoint a miscreant with sniper-like accuracy. His, "Boxsey, if you don't get that arm up shoulder high, I'll rip it off and slap you in the face with the soggy end!" became legendary.

We learned how to size off, tallest on the right, shortest on the left – right dress – form up in column of threes – march, march, march. It was good stuff and highly enjoyable – initially! There comes a time though, when enough is enough. Two weeks about did it for most of us!

Only another 17 months and two weeks to go...

I assumed my ATC training would help but that just goes to show how wrong some of us can be at times. The first time Tommy Temple saw me salute an officer the cadet way he nearly had a coronary.

"C'mere, son," he rasped, "who taught you to salute like that?"

"Air Training Corps, corporal," I beamed proudly, anticipating praise.

"Well, you're not in the Air Training Corps now, you're in the Royal Air Force and you'll salute properly – like this," and he threw up one of the crispest salutes I've ever seen.

"Now you try it," he ordered. Which I did. Time and time again, until he was happy. My arm was numb for hours afterwards.

"WHEN THE LEFT LEG GOES FORWARD, THE LEFT ARM ISN'T SUPPOSED TO GO WITH IT, YOU IDIOT AND WHEN I SAY ARMS SHOULDER HIGH, I DON'T MEAN LOFTY'S SHOULDERS JUST BECAUSE HE'S IN FRONT OF YOU!"

The drill session was going quite well I thought, seeing as how it was the first one. If you've never seen a squad being drilled for the first time, it's worth paying money to watch. Heels get trodden on, flailing arms are everywhere and the change step routine is amazing. When it's perfected, it can be carried out in a split second without too much disruption but when you've only just learned how to do it you can look like a pantomime horse with an exaggerated limp!

"WHEN I SAY 'STAND AT EASE,' IT DOESN'T MEAN YOU CAN FLOP ABOUT LIKE A TART AND WHEN I SAY 'BY THE RIGHT' IT DOESN'T MEAN YOU MOVE OFF ON YOUR RIGHT FOOT EITHER. YOU, COME OUT HERE AND DEMONSTRATE THAT MARCHING STYLE AGAIN – YOU LOOKED LIKE A COW WITH FROZEN TITS BACK THERE..."

Oh, the fun we had!

The discipline was unrelenting and we were on the move from reveille at 0600 to lights out at 2200. We learned how to bull our boots until they gleamed and our brasses (front and back) until they shone like crystal. The smell of boot polish and Duraglit became familiar odours that would stay with us for a very long time.

There was the odd disaster, naturally. To provide a smooth surface on the toes of new boots, in readiness for bulling, it was necessary to first get rid of the pimples. These pimples were merely thousands of tiny bumps that adorned the surface of the boot leather, but they were almost impossible to bull over. How then, to get rid of them? The answer is quite logical really.

You run a hot iron over them!

The knack however, was to ensure the iron wasn't too hot and that you didn't leave it on the leather too long. The choking smell of burning leather became another sensory memory of boy entrant training. Not to mention the state the irons used to get in – it was hell's own job trying to scrape molten leather off them!

Bed packs and hospital corners had to be in place every morning and these were a nightmare for most of us. To build a bed pack took careful folding abilities and an eye for detail. Sheets and blankets had to be stacked up carefully and wrapped neatly in another blanket. The stack would then be set at the head of the bead on top of the bedspread. This, in turn, would be stretched as taut as a bowstring over the mattress and folded into hospital corners at the foot of the bed. All this entailed was folding the bedspread under the mattress in such a manner that a ruler straight, diagonal crease formed to present a smart, eye-catching piece of domestic wizardry to the inspecting officer or NCO.

It should have been a doddle...

It wasn't – but it should have been...

My first bed pack looked like a squashed liquorice allsort and my hospital corners looked like crumpled socks! One or two smug, sad cases stood by immaculate beds but they were in the minority. The rest of us were forced to listen to our shortcomings whilst our bed packs were flung high in the air as an indication that they weren't up to expectations.

"WHAT – bedpack lifted off bed – DO YOU CALL – bedpack thrown at the ceiling – THAT – sheets and blankets cascading everywhere - ...AND DON'T TELL ME A BED PACK BECAUSE IT BLOODY ISN'T, IS IT?"

Well, pardon me for being born but I thought it wasn't a bad effort.

"No, Corporal." Trying to stay at attention with a blanket draped over your shoulder.

As if cleaning your kit and assembling bed packs wasn't enough, we all had rostered billet duties to perform day and night. The floor had to be polished to a high standard, toilets had to be sparkling, windows and brass window fittings had to be kept shining, everything needed dusting and, worst of all, the stoves had to be kept immaculate.

This was a job despised by all, comprising the cleaning out of the ashes from the previous night's fire and the complete 'blacking' of the whole stove. The blacking was a substance not unlike boot polish and it stank the billet out. When the stove was re-lit at night, the effect was one of mass asphyxiation. It was standard procedure for the lad who happened to be on stove cleaning duties to try and persuade everyone that we didn't need a fire in the evening. This happened even when icicles were hanging down from eyelashes, fire buckets were frozen solid and everyone was huddled into their greatcoats. The fire was lit anyway, so why we kept on about it, I don't know.

Mind you, when you managed to smuggle some bread and butter back to the billet, they were great for making toast! Even this innocent piece of thievery was fraught with danger though and if you happened to get caught swiping food from the mess, the consequences were dire. It was either stuck on a charge or fatigues. Every so often, you'd file in for tea and there'd be some poor sod stood on a chair in the middle of the mess chanting, "I am a thief – I steal bread and butter from the Royal Air Force, I am a thief – I steal bread and butter from the Royal Air Force..."

Talk about embarrassing.

There was never quite enough coal for these stoves to keep us warm in winter and someone plucked up the courage to ask Tommy Temple if we could have a little extra for our needs.

"No, you can't!" he barked. "Your allocation is all you'll get ... legally."

"Sorry, corporal?"

"Look, son, where's the coal bunker?" Tommy asked in a resigned manner, as though talking to somebody with learning difficulties.

"Over there, corporal, just across from the mess by the trees."

"Is it locked?"

"Yes, corporal."

"Has the coal bunker got a roof on it?"

"No, corporal." Light beginning to dawn…

"Well then?"

"Thank you, corporal."

The raid took place that night – it was the first of many and we never went short of coal again.

Polishing the floor was an education in itself. You couldn't just slap some polish down and rub it in any old how – not if you wanted to escape a major bollocking anyway. You had to get down on your hands and knees and perform small, circular movements with a polished rag. You also had to get rid of any marks you came across while you were at it and many a floor lackey found himself on fatigues for missing a quarter inch black mark hidden under a shadow somewhere.

When the polish was well and truly worked in, it then had to be buffed to a high shine and for this task we were provided with an incredible piece of equipment called a bumper. I pray that somewhere, someone has seen fit to preserve a bumper in a museum for future academics to puzzle over. What they'll make of it is anyone's guess but it's a safe bet they'll mark it down as an instrument of torture...

If they do, they won't be all that far off the mark!

I can only describe a bumper as a square lump of solid iron attached to a stout wooden broom handle. The handle was set in a flexible swivel that allowed the iron base to remain flat on the floor whilst it was hauled back and forth. Bumper pads were placed under the base and these took care of the polishing requirements. On inspection days, to keep the floor shiny and to prevent any accidental scuffing, everyone moved about with spare bumper pads under their feet.

The bumper was ungainly and dangerous in the wrong hands. Unfortunately, most of us had the wrong hands initially.

Strained muscles, blisters on the hands and crushed toes were standard operating hazards of the dreaded bumper.

You could work up a great shine with it though and it did wonders for underdeveloped shoulder muscles!

Each day would see us lined up in front of our huts prior to marching off to the days designated activities. Corporal Temple was moving slowly along the ranks one unforgettable day and I could hear him saying kindly (!) "Haircut – shave."

"Haven't started shaving yet, corporal," came from almost everyone, including me. His answer never varied:

"Start."

The following morning was carnage. There was blood all over the place as razor blade met delicate skin for the first time. Tommy Temple almost smiled as he surveyed the damage to our faces – almost!

God, did it sting...!

Life began to straighten itself out. We had a programme of trade training, education, physical education and other activities carefully mapped out for us. The education lessons didn't go down too well, as it was a bit like going back to school – which we hadn't long left! RAF Education Test Part One was an important milestone though and so we knuckled down as well as could be expected.

Trade training was a bit of a revelation. I didn't think there'd be a great deal to learn about store-bashing – just a few pointers about convincing somebody that the ill-fitting uniform they were trying on fitted like a glove. Either that or ensuring whatever went over the counter was signed for in triplicate – minimum! It took eighteen months to cover the complex supply structure of the Royal Air Force and even then it didn't all sink in. This was no reflection on our instructors though. Some of us were naturally gifted with a downward learning curve!

My attention span was very limited during some of these trade training sessions and I really hated it when a piece of chalk bounced off my torso and a yelling instructor shouted,

"WHAT HAVE I JUST SAID, BOY ENTRANT?" as I sat in a semi-coma staring out of the window.

A long silence usually followed whilst I frantically tried to recollect what had been said prior to the missile strike. The whole classroom looked on with bated breath. This was good sport if it was happening to somebody else.

"YOU HAVEN'T GOT A BLOODY CLUE, HAVE YOU?" usually followed, which was okay because I knew the answer to that one.

"No, Sergeant. Sorry."

"YOU WILL BE BLOODY SORRY WHEN YOU FAIL YOUR FINALS AND GET THROWN OUT. NOW DAMN WELL COME AND SIT HERE WHERE I CAN KEEP AN EYE ON YOU."

It hadn't occurred to me that I could get thrown out of the RAF if I failed my exams, but that was exactly what could, and did, happen to others. You could also get back-entried if you weren't keeping up with things, which meant dropping back an entry to go over the same ground a second time. Neither of these options appealed to me and I began to pay a lot more attention from that point onwards.

"The craving for sweet stuff was always with us and the long queues at the NAAFI counter didn't help. Nearly everyone stacked their plates up with cakes on pay day but, by the time we'd reached the single pay out counter, there'd be a lot of bulging bel-

*lies and not too many cakes left to pay for!" (**Bill Hodges**, 3 Sqn)*

Our uniforms duly turned up, along with our peaked caps with the red and white chequered hatbands denoting boy entrant status. On our left sleeves we wore the boy entrant wheel, a brass badge with a circular outer edge and a four bladed propeller inside. The wheel sat on top of a piece of circular, coloured plastic denoting our squadron (our number 3 squadron was green, 1 squadron red, 2 squadron blue and 4 squadron yellow). When we were eventually allowed out in public (after three months and, even then, only in uniform) those among us who had the good fortune to find a young lady to talk to, told them that these insignia indicated that we were trainee helicopter pilots!

Personally, I never found any young lady willing to talk to a lonely boy entrant. I guessed their parents might have had a hand in this matter at some stage, not to mention jealous local lads harbouring fearsome grudges.

Being regarded as lepers notwithstanding, we were now bonding together as one unit and lifelong friendships were being formed. Huts had their own loyalties but when we came together, it was a flight loyalty. If anyone faltered along the way, they were either helped or disciplined by their mates and sometimes we may have gone a bit over the top. Lack of hygiene resulted in the offender being slung in a freezing cold bath and scrubbed down with a stiff brush! On the other hand, if you had problems of a more practical nature, you could count on help from all quarters. I look particularly to the assistance provided to those who found themselves on jankers.

This form of punishment was meted out for offences deemed beyond those normally atoned for with fatigues. It was quite a harsh punishment and meant frequent parades outside the guardroom in full uniform and full webbing. Offenders would find themselves scrutinised from top to toe and then ordered to attend the next parade with all webbing scrubbed clean. At the next parade, they'd be told to attend the next one with all webbing fully blancoed etc etc etc. It was an almost impossible task, but with the webbing taken apart, divided amongst your mates, scrubbed or blancoed as required and re-assembled, it was easy.

We had boy entrants on jankers parades that would make a guardsman look sloppy!

The beginning was almost over. In most fields, it would have been a case of 'the worst is over,' but we weren't in any old field, we were in boy entrant training … and the worst was yet to come!

2.   Marching, Pecking Orders, Guns and Things

It wasn't just *a* parade ground and it wasn't just *the* parade ground. It was a piece of *holy* ground and it belonged exclusively to the drill NCOs. You didn't *walk* onto the parade ground – you *marched* onto the parade ground and, unless you were being carted off on a stretcher, you also marched *off* the parade ground.

How do I know all this? I'll tell you how I know all this.

Because I once walked on to the parade ground when Sergeant Thomas was drilling our flight, that's how. I'd only made about a hundred yards, when Sergeant Thomas's radar activated and he spun around to look in my direction.

I found it quite disconcerting, the range of emotions that swept across his face, so I broke into a trot, thinking this might please him.

It didn't!

"WHAT THE HELL DO YOU THINK YOU'RE DOING?" he bellowed, which threw me a bit because I thought it was fairly obvious what I was doing. I came to a halt and came to attention at the same time. I didn't answer him, as NCOs generally answer their own questions anyway, and waited for further developments.

I was quite frightened by this time!

"THIS IS MY PARADE GROUND, NOT A BLOODY PUBLIC PARK AND YOU WILL NOT STROLL ACROSS IT LIKE A VICAR. NOW GET OFF, ASK MY PERMISSION TO COME BACK ON AGAIN AND THIS TIME, BLOODY MARCH..."

Which I did. Very, very smartly.

We pounded that parade ground for eighteen months and became really good at foot drill. We had a few problems with rifle drill though...

"STAND AT – EASE!"

CLATTER! rifle on the ground.

"THE NEXT TIME THAT HAPPENS, YOU'D BETTER HIT THE GROUND BEFORE YOUR RIFLE, OR YOU'LL REGRET IT – UNDERSTAND?"

"Yes, corporal."

I didn't really understand the bit about hitting the ground before your rifle but was soon enlightened.

"It means, moron, that you will have fainted and had no control over the rifle when it hit the ground. If I ever see your rifle lying on the ground with you stood over it again, I'll send you to join it – understood?"

"Yes, corporal," very quietly.

The rifles were .303 Lee Enfields and they weren't light either. They were coming to the end of their service life and would shortly be replaced by the SLR but the Lee Enfield was the rifle we used for our basic weapon training in 1961. The first time we fired them, we discovered what it must have felt like to be kicked in the shoulder by a maddened stallion! The pile driving kick of the .303 was shudderingly painful and there was a lot of grunting, sobbing and swearing on the firing range before we took to folding our berets over, tucking them inside our shirts and using them as shock absorbers.

For drill purposes though, they were alright. Until you made a mistake on the parade ground...

Then it was rifle over your head and double around the square time. How many times depended on the severity of your mistake or the mood of your drill instructor. We learned quickly that way!

Then it was decided we'd try a little rifle drill with fixed bayonets and, once again, mayhem fell on our little world of woe.

"FIX – BAYONETS!"

"ATTEN – TION!"

CLATTER! at least two bayonets rattled noisily to the deck.

"YOU BLOODY IDIOTS etc etc...!"

One or two minor puncture wounds to the hands occurred and we heard that someone from one of the other squadrons had fainted and driven his bayonet into his shoulder when he sagged forward. Again, we learned our lessons and nobody stabbed themselves after that first performance. Naturally, when you place a lethal weapon in the hands of excitable youngsters, they immediately start looking around for something to use it on. The rifles were okay, as we got to fire them on the range but the Royal Air Force, in its wisdom, decided that we wouldn't be taught the art of bayonet fighting!

This was a huge disappointment, so where to find something to stab?

Toilet blocks (not our own, of course) provided the answer. A whole row of wooden cubicle doors just waiting to receive savage bayonet thrusts. We were formed up on the road leading to the parade ground one day and were just a few hundred yards from a toilet block. Everybody's sudden urge to relieve themselves surprised Tommy Temple but he allowed us to 'fall out' in relays. Once inside, a suitable door was singled out and severe harm inflicted. It looked like a chopping board afterwards! Roy went over the top though. He Thrust his bayonet in with such force that he couldn't get it out again. It took three of us to release it.

Apart from the .303 rifle, we received instruction on the Bren gun, another stalwart from the Second World War. The Bren was a machine gun and much kinder than the .303 rifle. It had no kick at all and even tended to pull forward when fired. It was a great favourite with all of us but had one draw-back. It couldn't be fired left handed because the sights were set on the left side of the gun. Sadly, I happened to be left handed. The first range session we attended with the .303, I'd lain down with the rifle tucked comfortably into my left shoulder and my legs splayed out to my right. The rest of the boys were all right handed and their legs were splayed out neatly to the left. This upset the range corporal (another hard nut from the R.A.F Regiment) and he addressed me thus:

"THERE'S ALWAYS BLOODY ONE, ISN'T THERE," he kicked my boot, none too gently, to disengage it from the legs of the lad to my right, "YOU'RE AN AWKWARD BASTARD AREN'T YOU, BOY ENTRANT – WHAT ARE YOU?"

"An awkward bastard, corporal."

"CORRECT. YOU'VE RUINED MY NICE NEAT LINE WITH YOUR BLOODY LEGS SPRAWLED OUT ALL OVER THE PLACE – WHAT HAVE YOU DONE?"

"Ruined your nice neat line, corporal."

"CORRECT."

As it turned out, I almost got my marksman's badge with the .303. To obtain this cherished crossed rifles badge, it was necessary to put five bullets in a group that could be covered by an old penny coin. I'd put four together in a close group but the fifth was slightly off. In fairness to the range instructor, he twisted that penny in every direction to try and cover the five bullet holes but he just couldn't manage it. It was very disappointing and I never came that close again. It was extra money as well, but the badge was more important at that age.

With the Bren gun, I couldn't hit a barn door, but we all had great fun firing off long bursts and pretending to be Al Capone. Until we were hauled up by the curlies that is...

"CEASE FIRING – CEASE FIRING," came a semi-hysterical scream.

"YOU DO NOT FIRE A BREN GUN LIKE THAT – I WANT SHORT BURSTS – RATATAT – RATATAT – RATATAT. NOW, LET'S TRY IT AGAIN."

RATATATATATATATATATATATATATATAATATATAT...!.

"CEASE FIRING – CEASE FIRING," voice now all full of angst, "YOU BLOODY IDIOTS etc etc etc..."

We were given a lesson on stripping and re-assembling a Bren gun on one occasion and this was stress at the highest level. The instructor was our very own R.A.F Regiment range instructor and he had a rare talent for delivering scorn. He'd arranged us all in a large circle, lying flat behind our Brens. He commandeered the centre of the circle and all we could see of him from our prone position were his legs. He carefully took us through the weapon stripping routine and bade us re-assemble the weapon on his instruction. We were doing quite well until I went awry with something at the complicated end. There was a dreadful silence as everybody waited for me to stop clattering about and I became aware of a pair of legs heading in my direction.

I began to sweat and frantically pulled and pushed at the offending piece of mechanism.

The legs came to a halt directly in front of me – I stopped pulling and pushing and started praying.

"Where're you from, son?" came the surprisingly calm question.

"Cardiff, corporal," I replied cautiously.

"That'll f***ing explain it then," he said crushingly, and went back to his position. There was a lot of suppressed sniggering and it took an age to ready myself for the next stage of assembly. During this part of the operation, I heard a gentle THUD! to my left and turned to see Bernie Carrier looking at me with a desperate half smile on his face. The barrel of his Bren lay in the grass where it had fallen.

Bernie had failed to secure the barrel and, when he lifted the Bren up into the firing position, it had slid with mesmerizing smoothness out of its housing and toppled noisily to ground!

The legs approached.

"Where're you from, son?" came the familiar question.

"Wiltshire, corporal," replied Bernie.

"That'll f***ing explain it then," he was informed.

Frankly, we preferred the shouting!

Bernie spent the rest of the lesson running around the square with the Bren held high over his head. He was nicknamed "Bren Gun Bernie," from then on!

Apart from learning the art of shooting, we received lectures on the grim business of nuclear war. These lessons were desperately boring and, to most of us, utterly pointless. If someone took it on themselves to deposit a 50 megaton hydrogen bomb on our heads, we reasoned, what earthly use could we make of a one piece fall out suit and a pair of dark glasses!

Sid certainly found it boring. He fell asleep, slumped over the folding table at the back of the classroom during a lesson. It was a hot, sunny day and we were all feeling the effects of heat and boredom. Fear of reprisals kept us awake.

The sort of reprisal meted out to Sid – he had the table kicked out from under him!

Other lessons of this nature were a little more interesting and one in particular, stands head and shoulders above all others. A lesson in first aid seemed innocent enough at the time and we were quite happy to learn that this lesson would take the form of a Canadian Air Force training film. Several years later, I was to see the same film again but with a marked difference. On that occasion we were warned solemnly of its content and offered the chance to leave the room if we felt we couldn't stomach the scenes it contained.

Man's service could be very soft sometimes!

As boy entrants, we weren't offered this luxury and the only ones who left the room were those who did so horizontally!

The film was horrendous! It depicted the crash of an aircraft in a remote area and dealt with the dilemma of a crew member faced with the task of treating his colleagues injuries. The film was in glorious Technicolor and the blood was copious. There were stomach wounds, pumping arterial wounds, snapped bones sticking out of limb wounds – it makes me ill just thinking about it. It was the most graphic film I've ever seen but at least we learned something from it...

Never to get involved in aeroplane crashes!

Corporal: Listen Rook! - If The Pilot Shouts Jump!
And You ask Why? - You'll Be talking to Yourself !!

❖ ❖ ❖

Characters were emerging rapidly and it became easy to
spot those who were destined for promotion. The promotion scale took the form of senior boy, leading boy,
corporal boy, sergeant boy, flight sergeant boy and warrant officer boy. Warrant officer boy was the pinnacle
and there was only one nominated from each entry.

Those of us in the rank and file (the hoi polloi) resigned ourselves to a life of taking orders whilst the
gifted went for glory. It was very much accepted by everybody as a fair assessment however and friendships
rarely seemed to suffer. At this stage though, even the
red lanyard of the senior boy hadn't appeared in our
ranks. We were still battling through our formative
weeks and beginning to get to grips with service life.
With the resilience of youth, we were shrugging off the

hardships and facing new challenges with determination. Some of the more painful challenges could have been avoided though...

Without exception, everyone had to put their name down for a sport. It wasn't an option. It was compulsory for three months. As the man with the clipboard stood in our billet, taking our names and preferred sport, Chris Boxsey piped up with, "No need to ask Taff what sport he'll be playing," he said to the assembled throng. Everybody laughed knowingly. Rugby, of course. I was a Welshman, wasn't I? All Welshmen play rugby, don't they?

As a matter of fact no, they don't. To be fair, I'd played wing forward in primary school and loved the game, but I wasn't very good at it – in fact, I was useless.

"Rugby for you then, Price?"

"You bet, corporal," I said with an enthusiasm I wasn't feeling. Ken 'Boots' Armson put his name down as well, but Ken could play rugby and went on to prove he could play it very well indeed, before we'd finished.

The practice match, to test our qualities, was a nightmare. I'd told the captain my position was open side wing forward, which sounded pretty knowledgeable. I failed to mention that I was all of nine years old the last time I'd played! It took about ten minutes for him to switch me to blind side wing forward and another five for him to re-position me at full back. He told me to keep out of the way as much as possible!

I took up fencing after that debacle!

Sport was very much favoured by the R.A.F and, if you were good enough to represent your station on three or more occasions, you'd be awarded sporting 'colours'. This took the form of a certificate and a blue lanyard, both of which were much prized. We were also given the opportunity to work towards our Duke of Edinburgh's Award during our training and again, a richly embossed badge was awarded to those who obtained the silver standard. This was worn low down on the left sleeve of our uniforms.

I may have been academically challenged, but I managed to end up with both awards and the captaincy of the fencing team before I was through. We had some very gifted sportsmen in the flight and it was always a pleasure to watch someone like 'Huck' Bain carrying out spectacular dives in the swimming pool or Norman Carver soaring over the pole vault bar. That was in the days before airbags too and it made you wince to see him thudding down into the sandpit. It was all good fun and, combined with the regular gymnasium sessions, it made us very fit in a short space of time. This was advantageous because reporting sick was frowned upon greatly!

It was a matter of pride to refrain from reporting sick unless you were terminally ill and it led to some ill-advised happenings. A suffering creature in our hut mentioned that he had a very large, painful boil on his leg and, before he knew what he was agreeing to, he'd been held down in a chair whilst a little bit of amateur surgery was carried out. The duty corporal had come into the hut midway through the operation, flinched at the sight of the blood and assorted secretions, and shouted at us to get him to sickbay immediately. There was quite a scene and the butchered one bore several grudges for a long time afterwards.

Sgt. : " Your Detention's Served Rook.
Now — CLEAR OFF!! "
Rookie: But - That's What I Was In Here For
In The First Place Sergeant !!

I tried the brave approach just once, coming unstuck in some style. I'd attended rifle drill one sun-drenched morning with a badly bruised and swollen thumb from an accident the night before. I hadn't gone sick, relying on Tommy Temple's compassion to see me through!

"I don't think I can manage rifle drill, corporal," I reported to him, "damaged my thumb last night." I held the discoloured, misshapen appendage up for his examination. It looked like a piece of slaughtered pork!

"Where's your sick note?" he barked.

"I haven't got one, corporal. I didn't go sick."

"Pick up your rifle and get back in line then," he snarled. I whimpered my way through that session, barely able to lift the rifle off the ground. On my next report, Tommy wrote about my rifle drill, "Poor, due to idleness!"

I went to see him about this miscarriage of justice and he heard me out very well.

"Life can be a bastard sometimes, lad," he told me, "The first thing you should learn about it is that it's never fair, so get on with it and the next time we do rifle drill, impress me, okay?"

This did absolute wonders for me and I threw that rifle about like a feather from then on.

"Rifle drill much improved," was on the next report.

Loved it, didn't I?

Corporal Boy, Johnny Cooper created his own bit of medical history when he attempted to bring a little discipline into off-duty hooliganism. Several of the lads from his billet were tear-arseing around the outside of the hut in noisy fashion and Johnny had decided enough was enough. He'd thrown open a window as one of the offenders ran by, stuck his head out and just managed to shout, "STOP F***ING ABOUT..." when the next boisterous youth sprinted by and slammed it shut again!

As Johnny was being stretchered out of the hut to the waiting ambulance, he raised a weakened hand and caught hold of Corporal Boy, Jock Sinclair.

"Look after the lads, Jock," he whispered valiantly.

This was a sad tale but perversely, Keithy Brooks, who only saw the funny side of things, was left to tell the story to those of us in the other huts who hadn't witnessed the proceedings.

By the time he'd finished, we were in hysterics!

Johnny Cooper was a straight character and was once overheard berating someone from another entry who'd tried it on by queue bashing one of our flight

"What're you standing up for him for, he's just a little runt," Johnny had been challenged.

"He might be a little runt," Johnny had countered, "but he's our little runt, so pack it in."

There was also an outbreak of some dreadful adolescent disease during our training and most of us came out in spots. Those of us afflicted had to pack our kit and get up to sick quarters for hospitalisation during the incubation period. We were in there for a couple of days and were glad to get out again. The caring medical staff used us as skivvies and we were forced to polish and bumper the ward floor for our keep. It was vital for us to sweat the fever out, they said and kept a straight face while they were saying it as well!

The only ray of light up at sick quarters came in the form of a WAAF nursing attendant nicknamed Sexy Lexy. There were very few females on camp (not that we got to see anyway) and Lexy was the object of many a juvenile fantasy. Listening to some of the brasher elements it could have been assumed that Lexy had been vigorously bedded on numerous occasions in the treatment room. Looking back, it's hard to imagine anything less appealing than a boy entrant with a short, back and sides haircut, dressed in shapeless denim overalls and weighted down with big boots. It's also safe to assume that the only enlarged part of a bragging boy entrant that saw any action, was the imagination!

Apart from Lexy, the only other female I talked to on camp was a WAAF pilot officer and that wasn't all that pleasant. In fact, it was very much a one sided conversation and I didn't come out of it too well at all.

I'd been walking down the main drag to the billet and saw, at some distance, a squadron leader walking towards me on the left side of the road. Slightly behind him, on the right hand side of the road, was the aforementioned WAAF pilot officer. To make matters infinitely worse, I spotted Tommy Temple behind both of them but some way back.

I did what we all did on these occasions – I went into frenzy mode! Who should I salute! I could see that the two officers were going to pass me almost simultaneously and I opted for the squadron leader, who was marginally in front. If I was quick enough, I planned to snap another salute to the pilot officer. I knew Tommy Temple was surveying the coming confrontation with marked interest and I just knew I was in a no-win situation.

I whipped up a smart salute for the squadron leader, snapping my head to the left in textbook fashion. He then threw me out of synch by wishing me good morning and, by the time I'd returned the compliment, all was lost.

"BOY ENTRANT, COME HERE!" screeched an incensed female voice. I stopped in my tracks, turned and marched the short distance back to the livid looking pilot officer. I came to attention in front of her and gave her my very best salute.

"DON'T YOU SALUTE OFFICERS WHEN YOU PASS THEM, BOY ENTRANT?" she raved.

"Sorry ma-am, but I'd just saluted the squadron leader and..."

"I'M NOT INTERESTED IN WHO YOU DID SALUTE, I'M MORE CONCERNED WITH WHO YOU DIDN'T SALUTE, DO YOU UNDERSTAND?"

She then gave me a severe bollocking of a sustained nature. When it was over, I apologised again, gave her another salute and continued on my way. Tommy Temple was fast approaching – another bollocking I felt sure.

"Embarrassing, isn't it, son," he grinned as he passed me by.

Sometimes, you could actually like that man!

When I later queried the protocol in situations where an officer passed you on either side, it was explained that all I had to do was salute whilst looking straight ahead. The salute would then be an acknowledgement of both parties. During the rest of my service career I never came across that situation again and, believe me, I tried!

Every junior entry billet had a member of the senior entry in residence, usually a leading boy. They'd be in overall charge of the hut and be responsible for discipline out of normal hours. Hut 191 had Leading Boy, Dave Brandon in charge and, at the time, he was suffering badly with a boil on the back of his neck. It was a painful affliction and took a very long time to heal. Obviously, he received all the sympathy you'd expect and was known throughout the hut as 'Leading boil' Brandon – behind his back, of course.

Dave spoke to us one evening and gave a word of caution. He, and the rest of the senior entry, were soon to finish their training and would be enjoying their passing out ceremony very shortly. The new senior entry would then take over after the traditional 'entry night' mayhem and become our very own 'bull masters.' This, as tradition bade, meant that each one of us would be adopted by a member of the senior entry and used as a skivvy. We'd have to go to their billets and clean their kit, bull their boots and generally make life easier for them. It was an accepted way of life and we knew that, when our turn came, we'd enjoy the same privileges. As it turned out, many of us didn't and it was mostly down to the way we were treated over the coming months.

Dave Brandon had warned us that our new senior entry contained some real hard cases in their ranks and that we could be in for a rough time.

How right he was.

It's difficult to view that particular side of boy entrant life in a light-hearted manner and I cannot accept any suggestion that the sort of behaviour we were subjected to was character building. Every one of us suffered, some a great deal more than others and it wasn't just the inconvenience of cleaning someone else's kit. That, I think, we could have accepted on a realistic level, along with the queue bashing.

What we couldn't accept, however, was the face of bullying violence that took over and it triggered some very nasty moments. One or two of the more outspoken characters in our flight received some sickening beatings and it led to some very nasty confrontations. Most of us suffered some violence during this time, yet it became just another short-term ordeal to tough out. Nobody reported it, nor looked to bring any one person to justice – not at that time anyway. Suffice to say that several enemies were made during this period and a not inconsiderable amount of hatred was generated by the violence. Very little compassion was demonstrated by either side and it all seems a little sad now. In fairness, quite a few of the senior entry lads did their best to protect some of us in one form or another but even they weren't immune to the violent element amongst them. I lift my hat to those who had the courage to try and shield us, no matter how ineffective it may have been.

When we eventually became the senior entry, most of us opted out of tradition and left the junior entry pretty much at peace.

We felt it was the least we could do.

We were allowed every other Sunday off and didn't take too kindly to the church parades on the alternate Sundays. Squadron Leader the Reverend Darbyshire, our padre (or 'sky pilot' as he was known) was a very enthusiastic officer and it certainly wasn't personal when a lot of us tried very hard to avoid his sermons. The parade couldn't be avoided but it was possible to duck for cover when we were dismissed to file into church. Providing we were back in time for re-assembly and the march back to our billets, all was well.

Sometimes.

It became a little like, 'The Great Escape' as boy entrants dived into toilet blocks and any other handy hiding place until the church doors had closed. It was a bit of a farce at times and many a cookhouse fatigue party was made up of re-captured boy entrants who'd failed to evade NCO search parties.

"ALRIGHT, OUT! ALL OF YOU," Tommy Temple at the door of the church toilet block, "..AND YOU, GET OFF

THAT BLOODY ROOF BEFORE I COME UP THERE AND THROW YOU OFF...!"

There'll be some questions to answer when we get to the pearly gates!

Sundays were to take on a whole new meaning for us later on and we were to discover a brand new place to plead with the lord for deliverance and mercy. There were no hiding places there either...

The Brecon Beacons.

'A' Flight, No.3 Squadron, 43rd Entry RAF Hereford.

The author, Brian and Roy. The 'Astra' cinema is in the background.

'Bren Gun' Bernie (left) and Roy Mason with the author.

"I'm not going up in one of those things again!"

Chipmunk flight trainer.

The 1961/1962 R.A.F Hereford Fencing Team.

The inhabitants of Hut 191.

The Bren was a light machine gun and much favoured by boy entrants.

It was kind to their shoulders!

The Lee Enfield .303 rifle. When fired, its pulverising kick was extremely fierce and led to many a sobbing curse from badly bruised boy entrants.

"Let's try it lying down – bound to be easier."

5 star accommodation kept the rain out on Dartmoor but not the cold!

A moment's rest on Dartmoor. Sgt Carl Graffham is far left and Tap' Tappenden is far right.

The lads posing for another picture on Dartmoor.

Wheels Up!

3. Hot Sweet Tea and Aching Feet

"So where's the Brecon Beacons then?" some geographically challenged idiot asked me. There you go again – I was a Welshman, so I'd know where Brecon was situated. In fact, I'd never been there and only had a rough idea of its location.

I jerked a thumb vaguely to my left and told him it was just over that way somewhere, a bit north of Cardiff! He seemed happy enough with this and remarked that it sounded quite a nice place. He didn't like the sound of the Black Mountains though.

"Sounds a bit ominous to me" he opined.

"Killers," I said with authority, "One minute, nice and sunny then, Wallop! Blizzards, fog, freezing rain, avalanches, sheep stampedes…!"

The first time we went to the mountains, it was a bit of a breeze and led a lot of us into thinking any further trips would be equally easy. As the other excursions took the form of elimination marches for teams to represent R.A.F Hereford at the Ten Tors Dartmoor endurance race later on in the year, that first trip didn't even scratch the surface.

Ten Tors was a seriously tough contest and only a few out of the hundreds who first entered made the teams. Eddie Edwards and Ginger Troughton made it from our flight and that was no mean feat by anybody's standards. Out of the 225 teams who actually started Ten Tors in 1962, only 83 finished. Four of the teams from Hereford came in 1st, 2nd, 9th and 10th in their age group.

Every single boy entrant in the Hereford teams finished the course.

The first outing to Brecon started with breakfast in the mess and the issuing of packed lunches. These never varied. Corned beef sandwiches, cheese sandwiches and hard tack biscuits were our staple 'mountain' diet. Urns of very hot, very sweet tea were set out in the mess and, whatever it did to our teeth, it certainly boosted our energy levels. It was an amazing brew and absolutely delicious. A couple of cups of this, we thought, and we'd fly over those mountains. Well, okay, perhaps not fly, but hammer along at a cracking pace certainly; funny how the young can delude themselves with such absolute faith.

Mountains aren't vindictive, nor are they bent on destroying all those who dare set foot on them. In fact, they couldn't care less who traipses all over them and certainly wouldn't entertain crippling poor, suffering boy entrants for having the bloody cheek to challenge their superiority. I mention this because there were quite a few boy entrants at the end of the day that had this very thought in mind!

Blisters, sprains, stitches, stubbed toes – you name it, we had it. To cap it all, when we got back to base, 4 Squadron, (who were getting their first taste of field cooking) weren't quite ready to dish up dinner.

The uproar was out of all proportion really. I feel quite ashamed now, that I took part in all the shouting and flinging about of insults. It didn't take too long at all to learn that the very last people in the world you want to be upsetting are service cooks – especially those who're likely to be cooking your next meal!

When we returned to Brecon to begin the Ten Tors elimination tests, it was a different kettle of fish altogether and this time it was all about stamina and will power. One good, long push over the mountains would have been a lot easier than the soul-destroying method used to sort out the wheat from the chaff. We were hauled over the designated route for mile after bone wearying mile until we came back to our point of departure and the welcome sight of our transport back to base. There'd be that wonderful tea waiting for us and a flop down to soak up the feeling of sheer luxury generated by taking the weight off our feet. The unwise took off their boots.

Twenty minutes later we'd be offered the chance to stay on the transport or get back on our feet and do the same route again. The sheer, mental torture of this dilemma was dreadful. When all we wanted was to be left alone with our tea and throbbing feet, it couldn't even be considered. On that first outing, everybody dragged himself up and set out for the second time.

It was to be the last time that everybody finished the course.

The second test march was amazing and I'll carry two memories of it to my grave. We'd finished the first, long leg and were just setting off for the second trip. We had a PTI (physical training instructor) in charge of our team by the name of Corporal 'Bronco' Lane and he cheerfully told us that we'd be 'doubling' for part of the route! In fairness, he accepted that this was perhaps a little unreasonable when we were climbing up the mountains but he couldn't see any reason why we shouldn't run along the top and then down the other side. It would, he said, be a lot quicker than walking.

We disagreed but didn't mention it.

My first memory is of the whole squad doubling along the top of this huge mountain and seeing one of the lads stumble and fall to his knees a few positions ahead of me. His mate behind him reached down as he ran past, grabbed hold of the back of his webbing belt and pulled him up and forward with hardly a check in his stride. It happened in a matter of seconds and I doubt anybody ahead of us even noticed. If they didn't, then it's a shame.

The second memory came later on. We'd doubled headlong down a mountain slope and were fighting our way, gasping for breath, up the side of another unsmiling monster. Bronco was already half way up, whilst the rest of us were strung out behind him in disarray. I was somewhere near the back, head down and whimpering for deliverance, when I stumbled across Sid. He was flat on his back in the gorse and appeared to have lost a great deal of interest in life in general. I stopped and fell to my knees beside him. Not because I was all that concerned about him, more that I could take a rest whilst appearing to help a comrade in need!

"Come on, Sid, you can't stay there," I gasped, praying that he would – I didn't want to get off my knees just yet!

"Leave me alone, Taff, I wanna die," he groaned.

"WHAT'S GOING ON DOWN THERE?" bellowed Bronco from on high.

"It's Sid, corporal – he says he wants to die," I explained.

"WELL, TELL HIM HE CAN'T DIE YET AND THAT'S AN ORDER, SO GET HIM ON HIS FEET," came the uncaring reply.

"He says you can't die yet, Sid," I told the corpse-like figure lying before me.

"Oh! F***ing *hell!*" he managed to whisper as he struggled to his feet. Together, we cursed our way to the top of yet another mountain. I think more than two of us would have called it a day at that stage but Bronco had already warned us that no-one – repeat – no-one, would be allowed to drop out of his squad under any circumstances.

...And you couldn't really bring yourself to disappoint someone like corporal Bronco Lane!

...Unless you were tired of living!

The numbers dwindled rapidly during the further outings and I fell by the wayside on the penultimate test. I just about fell into the bus after the first stage of the trek and knew I was finished. I couldn't have moved if the bus had caught fire! Several of the lads who set off on the second stage dropped out along the way. They'd simply walked themselves to a standstill.

Those who went on to form the Ten Tors teams were, without a doubt, the very best the R.A.F could offer.

Dartmoor came next. They transported everybody down there, including other entries and flung us on the moors with wild abandon. We were put into teams of six and then paired off, as we'd be sleeping in two-man tents during the expedition. In addition to our heavy backpacks, we'd be taking it in turns to carry the tent. Lady luck favoured me for a change, teaming me up with Barry 'Tap' Tappenden, a big, genial lad I was to meet up with again during a tour of duty in Malaya.

"Give us that tent, Taff," he'd say on more than one occasion when I was wavering about all over the place.

Tap, I remembered thinking as the weight was lifted from my shoulders, was a prince among men!

The first part of the expedition took the form of a seventeen-mile hike in the Princetown, Nuns Cross, White Barrons area of South Dartmoor and we spent the night at Avon Dam (near Smallbrook Plains). The second part took us thirty two miles from Avon Dam to Cross Furzes, Powder Mills and through to Cator Court near Widecombe-on-the Moor. We spent two nights at Cross Furzes and Powder Mills.

Somewhere along the route, we tried to murder a chicken!

Four or five of us had gone out in the evening for a wander about and came across the chicken in a quiet country lane. A brief discussion took place and Bob Wetherill confirmed that he could pluck and clean it if someone could catch and kill it. I thought I could handle that without too much grief and decided that, if I could get close enough, I could kill it by using my webbing belt as a club (brass ends to the front). Creeping up on a wary chicken is no easy feat but I managed to get within swinging distance and drew my arm back for the killer swing.

WHOOOOSHHHH! About halfway down the swing, the chicken flew into the air with a manic screech and went straight through the nearest hedge. We were left with numerous feathers floating silently on the evening air.

"Ah! For Christ's sake..."

"You bloody cretin..."

...And so on.

I ate alone that night.

It wasn't roast chicken either!

During our time on Dartmoor, the Royal Marines invited us over to try out their assault course and this was accepted with boyish enthusiasm. We couldn't wait to get at it but, as usual, enthusiasm outweighed caution and casualties occurred.

Part of the course had us swinging, Tarzan style, into a large rope net and this proved highly entertaining. The approved method, as pointed out by friendly Royal Marine instructors, was to let go of the swinging rope as you approached the net and fall into it spread-eagled. This allowed you to grab hold of the net and scramble over it towards the next obstacle. I was towards the back of the course and saw all that went before me, which wasn't as advantageous as it sounds. The first thing I witnessed was Ginger Troughton doing his hair-raising best to imitate Superman. He'd let go of his rope swing when he was still a good eight feet from the net and literally flew into its embrace with arms and legs akimbo. It was spectacular if nothing else.

The next one to try it failed to let go of the rope, put both his legs through the net and hung there like a trapped fly in a spider's web whilst everybody fell about laughing. The course was quite hairy, being high up in the air for starters and one or two found themselves frozen to the horizontal ladder as it swayed alarmingly beneath them. The problem with this piece of apparatus lay in the fact that you needed to look down to locate the rungs. It meant, basically, that you also happened to notice the ground, a long, stomach lurching way down!

"COME ON, COME ON, STOP PRATTING ABOUT UP THERE. IF I'D WANTED YOU TO STOP AND TAKE IN THE SCENERY, I'D HAVE PUT A F***ING DECK CHAIR UP THERE FOR YOU!"

Somebody muttered something about marines being funny bastards but I was favouring the 'praying to God' option at the time and didn't take a lot of notice!!

The last obstacle to overcome was a thick rope that led from the treetops to the safety of the ground. All we had to do was shin down it and we'd be safe again. Nearly all of us made it; then Roy lost his grip and slid all the way down the rope. His hands were in a dreadful state and his language was shocking. It's a good job Royal Marines aren't easily offended!

There was an appalling test of nerve and balance to follow the obstacle course and this took the form of a very long rope stretched high and wide over a river. The idea was to lie flat with one foot hooked over the rope behind you and inch yourself forward until the river had been crossed. It looked terrifying when we got to it and it was with immense relief that I heard someone say the marines had called a halt to this exercise. When I looked down into the river, I could see a couple of out-ward spreading ripples with floundering bodies in the middle of them. It was a long drop and the ripples were very large! Apparently, the marines considered it a safe bet that the rest of us would end up floating down the river and didn't relish the thought of a wet rescue opera-tion.

There was a chorus of disappointment and protest from among the psycho element of course and one even ventured to ask the Royal Marine in charge of the course why we couldn't give it a go.

"Because," he replied with deep restraint, "you little bastards are scary enough when you're dry!"

Not content with exhausting and terrorising us, the powers on high decided we'd be given an initiative test to prove what out and out swine they could be when they felt like it. We were to go out in teams, at timed intervals, to navigate a set route. The 'initiative' came in the form of a large, square tin full of hard tack biscuits that had to be carried, stretcher-like, on two long poles. The tin was heavy and very awkward. Our team was the last out of base camp and we were discussing our best options when Padre Darbyshire came running over. It was a Sunday morning and he'd been preparing for his service when he realised nearly everyone had disappeared.

"Made it," he gasped as he skidded to a halt, "Corporal, can you delay their departure for an hour. They're all I've got left for a church parade."

It was the smallest church service I've ever attended but the padre was happy and even praised our singing at the end!

It wasn't easy, carting that biscuit tin about and it wasn't long before various suggestions were being made to ease our burden. Suggestions like eating some of the biscuits (too many of them), throwing them away (the tin would be checked at the other end) and even thumbing a lift on a lorry. We didn't get far with that little ploy and eventually; we had to settle for a simple, hard slog.

"So much for doing our Christian duty for the padre then," somebody whined, "I mean, how's about a bung of divine intervention to make this bloody biscuit tin a bit lighter!"

I can only imagine that the good lord has been asked many favours over the years but I'll lay odds that he's never been asked to make a biscuit tin a bit lighter before!

Back at Hereford once again, the usual programme of events carried on as before and life went on as only life could go on during boy entrant training. Leave came and went and concerned parents discovered, through inadvertent slips of the tongue, that their little boys had learned to swear whilst serving in Her Majesty's Royal Air Force!

Sadly, we were still too young to take our dads out for a drink down the pub. We could smoke though – we even had signed passes to confirm we'd reached the legal age of sixteen and were authorised to smoke. I didn't take advantage of this and never smoked during my days at Hereford, but most of the others did and it became one long round of scrounging fags until payday. The craving always outweighed the means however and one or two non-smoking entrepreneurs started up a little scam that kept them in pocket money for quite a while.

"They'd buy cigarettes and sell them on for three pence each to desperate addicts," one of the boys remembered.

"The money would be totalled up and paid out when the lads had plenty of leave pay to throw around. One of these bright sods came unstuck though. He thought he'd make a killing by buying up hundreds of really cheap herbal cigarettes and flogging them on for the same price as the dearer, brand smokes. The trouble was, these fags were so foul, he couldn't even give them away in the end. He was way out of pocket but at least he had a locker full of fags – shame he didn't smoke!"
(Paul Kinshott, 3 Sqn)

Winter brought a few memorable moments into our lives, some happy and some not so happy. On the plus side, hut 191 won the Christmas competition for the best decorated hut. We were presented with a wonderful Christmas cake and promptly made pigs of ourselves before even a photograph could be taken. There was a lot of muttering and snide remarks from the other huts, but we just didn't care.

The night before the judging of this competition, Lofty had been tasked with selecting several volunteers to stay and decorate the hut whilst the rest went up to the new block for an evenings 'bulling.' As was to be expected, he was inundated with volunteers and opted to go for the favouritism option. We all had our particular mates during training and our little circle included Lofty, myself, Bernie, Roy, Brian and Charlie Gibson. We were all selected and a lot of jeering and sniping followed, which affected Lofty not a lot! Everybody was allocated nice little jobs, like hanging up the trimmings or decorating the tree and I was congratulating myself with avoiding all that hard work up at the new block, when...

"Taff, you can polish and bumper the floor," Lofty told me, and I was livid. My protestations affected him about as much as the jeering and sniping had and I spent the rest of the evening working like a galley slave. Bernie felt obliged to show a bit of solidarity, being my best mate, but he kept it pretty muted in case he ended up alongside me! The floor was like a mirror afterwards and I was just about exhausted when the rest of the lads came back from their labours up at the new block. Every one of them used a set of bumper pads to keep it shiny for the judging.

We won hands down and went about, insufferably smug, for days afterwards.

On the minus side of winter, there was a mini riot one night, with one of the lads doing some damage to a bit of another entry's property. It was a freezing night, with snow on the ground and, although we'd all managed to get into bed, our billet had been identified as the vandal's lair.

A lot of screaming and shouting followed and we were ordered outside to form up – in our pyjamas. Everybody managed to get their boots on and grab great coats but it was freezing cold stood out there whilst a hollering NCO threatened to keep us there all night if the offender didn't own up. Nobody moved an inch and this decided the issue. Loyalty works two ways and the right thing for the offender to do, would have been to step forward to spare his mates from a long ordeal.

He chose not to and negated the need to be shown loyalty in return. From the ranks of frozen boy entrants, he was propelled violently forward by several hard shoves in the back!

Then we were dismissed and went back to bed.

Nobody had a guilty conscience!

The gas chamber came next, a little exercise we all wanted to avoid. Luckily, I did. I was away fencing when the rest of the lads were marched up to the chamber and ordered to put on gas masks. I understand it wasn't funny although Tommy Temple tried to lighten matters up by telling Charlie Gibson to take his mask off when it was already off!!!

"They made us take our bloody masks off in there, Taff," I was told. "Then they told us to give our last three numbers and name to prove we were okay. How the f**k? could we be okay? Heaving our lungs out, weren't we?"

I was very glad that I'd missed being gassed. Mind you, I made out I was bitterly disappointed at the time. Justice prevailed several years later though, when I took part in a riot demonstration with the R.A.F Regiment in Malaya. I'd been part of the rioting mob and was having a wonderful time throwing tomatoes and flour bombs at the lads when things took a turn for the worse. Several canisters flew over our heads and clattered to the ground behind us, emitting what I thought was smoke. The troops then charged and drove us back into the dense cloud that I quickly discovered was tear gas. I then learned why the boys at Hereford didn't find the experience 'funny.'

Regular billet and kit inspections kept us all on our toes and these often went into the realms of incredulity. The inspecting officer would poke a match into the corner of a locker, scratching for dirt, or run a white-gloved hand over every surface available, looking for dust. Whilst all this was going on behind us, all we could do was stand to attention at the foot of our beds, face front, and pray like crazy.

A regular trauma for me came courtesy of 'Manxy', whose bed space was directly opposite mine. Manx had problems with a stutter at the time and the letter 'F' seemed to give him the biggest problem. By a cruel twist of fate, Manx's service number was 1944444. As the inspecting officer came up to each bed space, we had to come to attention, give our last three numbers, rank and name. I'd be facing Manx as his turn approached.

It was agonising!

His face would contort into a variety of shapes as he fought to get his number out and, more often than not, the inspecting officer would take a quick look at the name on the locker and say, "Alright, Matthews, that'll do, son."

Manx only had problems when confronted by this sort of dilemma and, if justice ever prevailed, someone must have changed his number at some stage of the game.

Then again, probably not!

There was a strict code of practice in the billets that never varied. Whenever anyone in authority entered the hut, the first person to spot him would shout out, "NCO IN THE BILLET," or "OFFICER PRESENT," and everyone would immediately stop what they were doing and jump to attention by their beds. This wasn't a problem and our reactions were quickly honed – which was just as well when the dreaded 'hut raid' strikes occurred. Raiding parties from the senior entry would burst through the front and back doors of the hut, systematically grab the bottom of each bed in turn and hurl it upright against the wall.

Depending on your re-action time, it meant either standing forlornly alongside an upended bed or being suffocated by it as it pinned you to the wall!

Even the hut raids paled alongside the feared foot inspections however and these usually took place when you were fast asleep in the early hours of the morning.

Being dragged out of deep slumber by loud shouting and blazing lights isn't all that pleasant and when you realise it's a foot inspection, it's even worse. Frantic thoughts about when you last washed your feet raced to mind and a terrible dread settled on your soul if you couldn't remember.

"LOOK AT THE STATE OF YOUR FEET," someone nearby was bawled at, "GET OUT HERE AND LET EVERYBODY HAVE A LOOK AT WHAT YOU CLIMBED INTO BED WITH, YOU FOUL AND DISGUSTING CREATURE."

We all took a look and agreed with the inspecting corporal that the offending feet were indeed suitable for planting potatoes in, then moved back to await our turn. Without exception, offenders would be placed on a charge and I venture to suggest that quite a few of us carried a clean feet fixation about with us for a very long time afterwards!

> "I'll never forget those inoculations, nor being marched up en masse to wait in line for them. We were injected in alphabetical order and rumour had it that they used the same needle for whole flights. Those of us way down the alphabetical list were convinced the needle would be as blunt as a used nail by the time we took our turn."
>
> "It wasn't unusual to have jabs in both arms and they'd be sore for ages. Tommy Temple's idea of a cure was to march us back to the billet with arms swinging shoulder high!" (**Bob Wetherill**, 3 Sqn)

I still don't know what all those injections were for and I have a pet theory that trainee medics used boy entrants for needle familiarisation lessons. We had two at once on one occasion, in each lower forearm and they stung like crazy. When I joined the rest of the lads outside, they were lolling about on the grass holding their arms and telling horror stories.

"Did you see the way that prick from 2 Squadron fainted? WALLOP! Straight down – hell of a thud."

"Yeah, and what about that medic. He closed his eyes when he stuck that needle in me."

"If Temple thinks I'm going to march back with arms shoulder high after that, he's got another f***ing think coming!"

Yeah, right!

Civvy Street seemed a million miles away by now and it surprised me how quickly we adapted to our new way of life. Apart from the odd rumble of discontent from the odd malcontent, we were moving onwards with optimism, looking forward to our futures, whatever they were to hold for us. As predicted at the outset, we started to lose some of our flight members along the way. Apart from one Scots lad from the Outer Hebrides who left before signing on, (he also tried to talk Haggis Gibson into leaving with him – some sort of clan thing probably!) we lost one to another squadron, one back-entried to try again and one genius called Gloucester, to another trade.

Gloucester had a photographic memory and surprised everyone with his consistently high test results. He'd often be seen lying on his pit, reading comics while the rest of us pored over our trade manuals with deeply furrowed brows. He was a big, ruddy-cheeked lad with a slow Gloucester drawl and gave the impression that he might have been a bit slow on the uptake – which just goes to show how deceptive appearances can be. It wasn't long before the R.A.F recognised his talents and he was posted out of camp to higher things (Rocket scientist, someone suggested!).

The rest hung in there with varying degrees of desperation and looked forward to the next distraction.

Rookie: " Reporting Sick Corporal "
Corporal: "Fall in Rook - And As it's Such a Cold, Chilly
    Morning We'll all Double to Sick Quarters "

4.   Flying, Flapping and Showing Off

"FLYING! THEY WON'T SEND US FLYING. WHERE'D YOU THINK WE ARE – IN THE R.A.F?"

Sarcasm notwithstanding, we were indeed going flying and it meant piling aboard those good old three-tonners once again, for the long haul to a station that actually had aeroplanes. Chipmunks to be exact, two-seater training aircraft that had a tendency to bounce around a bit if the wind was just above half a knot!

Bernie was looking forward to it though, as he'd agreed to come on a gliding holiday with me on our next leave and had never flown before. I'd already flown in a Chipmunk with the ATC and considered them the best thing since brown sauce, whilst Malc Gallavan raved about their aerobatic qualities and couldn't wait to get on the outside of an inverted loop! Tom Nolan was a bit more laid back about it all though – at sixteen, he was already a qualified glider pilot.

The long journey from Hereford in the three-tonners was a lumbering ordeal and more than one suffering traveller was heaving over the lorry's tailgate before we reached the airfield. On arrival, flying didn't seem such a good idea after all!

"How's that – comfortable?" asked the airman strapping our parachutes on.

"Yes, thanks," we replied

"Oh, really – can't be tight enough then," he responded and proceeded to try and break our voices by hauling on the crotch harness so hard that we were left doing a fairish impression of Quasimodo! We then had to get from the hangar to the aeroplane, walking like orang-utans with sciatica!

Bets were being taken as to who'd raise the biggest laugh from watching airmen!

There's a wonderful, unique feeling about a light aircraft's cockpit and a comforting odour of rubber, oil and seat leather. I was strapped in the back seat and a cloth helmet was pulled over my head. The mouthpiece was clipped on and I was instructed how to use it to speak to the pilot. My safety drill, in the event of an air emergency, came from the pilot and this, I felt, was worth listening to.

"In the event of an emergency requiring us to exit the aeroplane, I will slide back the canopy and instruct you to climb out on to the wing. I will then shout, JUMP, JUMP twice and you will exit the aircraft immediately. If you hear this word a third time, it won't be me saying it because I won't be there anymore, okay?"

Afterwards, this line seemed very funny indeed, but I didn't find it at all funny at the time!

We started to roll forward and I couldn't wait to get up in the air. At last, I was going to fly as a member of the Royal Air Force.

The engine noise increased and we began to pick up speed, the ground speeding by beneath. The bouncing about suddenly stopped and we were airborne, clawing skywards with that wonderful feeling of release. I watched fascinated, as the ground fell away and the patchwork quilt appearance of countryside fields lay out beneath us. This was good stuff and a strong feeling of superiority began to creep over me. I was flying and couldn't be touched by earthbound worries and problems until we were back on the ground. I have never lost this sense of freedom whilst flying but must admit that modern aircraft aren't high on my list of 'favourites.'

"If it hasn't got a propeller, it ain't a aeroplane," I was once told and I'm more than happy to support this theory. The DC3, to me at least, is the greatest aeroplane that has ever been, or ever will be, constructed.

"Okay," came the pilot's voice over my headset, "we've got a nice bit of height now, so what would you like to do?"

"Can I fly the aeroplane, sir," I asked hopefully.

"Not a problem," he replied, "hold the stick lightly and put your feet on the rudder pedals. Try a few gentle turns."

When I had control, I was away with the fairies and started in on some spectacular turns and dives. My pilot, to his eternal credit, let me get on with it and only took over when I'd lost nearly all the height he'd so patiently gained.

"Anything else," he asked.

"Yes, Sir, what causes 'G'," I asked. I was really interested in this phenomenon and wondered how it came about. I'd seen a film where the pilot's face had become all distorted with the pressure of a steep dive and it fascinated me.

I'd have been quite happy with a verbal explanation but no, this wouldn't do for the cream of the Royal Air Force would it? A practical demonstration just had to be laid on, didn't it?

I can remember the aircraft taking on a high, nose up attitude whilst banking to the right and I can vaguely remember it slamming violently over to the left and diving steeply. After that, things became a bit blurred and I couldn't breathe!

"Does that explain things, or would you like to go through it once again?" came from somewhere like a million miles away, over my headset.

Not a bleeding chance, sunshine – are you trying to kill me up here, or what...

"No thank you, sir, that's perfect!"

I kept my mouth shut after that little scenario and enjoyed the rest of the flight immensely. I was more than a little sorry when we landed.

Bernie, who hadn't been too well in the three-tonner, came over to me for a confidential chat. He looked a bit ashen. It seems his pilot had got a bit bored and, without so much as a, "By your leave," to Bernie, had executed three rapid barrel rolls on the trot.

"If it's all the same to you, Taff, I don't think I'll come on that gliding holiday after all!" he told me.

Roy Mason came with me instead.

At least we managed to get in the air. The weather had closed in when the rest of the flight turned up – they were taken swimming instead!

My daughter once asked me what I remembered about the start of the swinging sixties and it took a while for me to come up with an answer. I remember we had a tannoy system in the new blocks that was linked up to the R.A.F Hereford amateur radio station and it was here that I began to pick up a little knowledge of the current music scene. It was all very much in the background though, until some bright spark invited special record requests from boy entrants.

It sounded a great idea. Give the little brats a treat and make them feel welcome on this planet by encouraging their musical appreciation of things melodic.

It didn't happen that way though, did it? That was far too straightforward for boy entrants. I remember the very first request being read out by a mock-serious DJ.

"...and now, for all the lads in the junior entry, from your mates in the senior entry – Roy Orbison and 'Running Scared!'

That was it. Everyone had to get in on the act after that and we had, 'Climb every Mountain' for all those who failed the Ten Tors tests on Brecon and various other inflammatory requests, designed to infuriate somebody or other.

Cliff Richard was doing his broody, mysterious bit at the time and Bas Thorley had a fair old bash at his style in the camp concert. One or two girls actually screamed at him, but we put that down to too much sherry before leaving home!

We had our own musicians in the boy entrant band of course and, although they were a bit limited in their choice of music, they still managed to punch out a decent tune now and again. The sound of drums and bugles at breakfast time on a cold, wet morning didn't exactly encourage a deep appreciation of military music but it cheered us up no end to see the band dripping wet and frozen to the marrow as they strove to master heroic marches.

Swinging sixties?

Tell me about the swinging sixties.

The camp cinema (the Astra) was showing Dr No with Sean Connery as James Bond and this was good stuff. It was just the sort of thing to fire up the imagination for the next time we were on the firing range and many an aspiring secret agent wished fervently that his last three service numbers were 007.

Bob Wetherill enjoyed a trip to the pictures as much as the rest of us, but he had a bit of a thing about the pre-show musical entertainment. Before the start of every film we ever saw, the theme music from 'A Summer Place' filled the cinema with its dreary melody, rising to a crescendo of mind numbing banality to just about numb the senses.

"I hated that bloody tune," he told me recently, "In fact, I hate it to this day!"

The hardships we had to endure, and I haven't even mentioned trying to get outside the cinema before 'The Queen' was played at the end of every performance!

Bill Hayley was still rocking around the clock and Elvis was thrusting his pelvis about like a man possessed, yet it didn't really register as history in the making. Lofty brought some Buddy Holly records back from leave on one occasion and gave us an insight into his enthusiasm for this tragic singer. I think Lofty mourned his passing with a genuine sense of loss for the music that could have been.

Roy, on the other hand, brought back a recording of Johnny Unitas winning a last gasp game of American football for his team! Roy's dad had flown in B17 Flying Fortresses in the war and had settled in England at the end of hostilities. He managed to pass on his love of American football to his son who, in turn, tried to pass it on to everyone else!

"SLOOWWW – MARCH. Don't let your foot pause, follow through evenly, don't lose the step – DON'T BLOODY CHANGE STEP IN SLOW MOTION, YOU IDIOT..."

We thought we knew all there was to know about foot drill until it came to the slow march. Tommy Temple told us that chimpanzees moved with more grace and co-ordination than we did and if we didn't want to spend all night on the parade square, we'd better get a bloody grip – etc, etc, etc!

It wasn't easy but we had to master it before our passing out parade and this was no longer impossibly far away. What had once seemed like a wistful dream, was now only a few short months ahead. Before this longed for milestone could be reached however, there was the little matter of passing our final exams. Fail them and there'd be no passing out parade.

There were quite a few sweaty palms as we studied for our finals and ducking out of church parades became a little more serious. Those who managed it, went straight to the classrooms for a couple of hours extra study. Maybe this'll go in our favour at the Pearly Gates!

"ORDER – ARMS. SLOPE – ARMS. PRE-SENT – ARMS," over and over again until we were inch perfect. Then we did it all again in greatcoats because our passing out parade would be in December. This also ranked fairly high on the not funny scale, as greatcoats aren't the most flexible of garments and It felt a bit like doing drill in a straightjacket. Add a tight fitting webbing belt and it was little short of a miracle that we could even move, let alone march with rifle and bayonet!

March we did though, day in and day out until it became second nature. We stomped to attention when we addressed an NCO and it was always, "Corporal," or "Sergeant." It was NEVER, "Corp," or "Sarge".

It would have been like using their Christian names!

Which wouldn't have been at all wise!

When the 42nd entry left, we became the senior entry and prepared for our 'entry night' celebrations. These entry nights could only be described as pagan festivals, whereby those in the senior entry generally ran amok. Providing we didn't do too much damage to property or junior entry however, those in command generally cast a blind eye. We queue bashed in the mess and took over the senior entry room in the NAAFI, enjoying ourselves immensely. Later on, walking back to the billet, a few of us came across a gaggle of lads from another squadron who were industriously pushing a car down the road.

"Who's car's that?" we asked.

"No idea! Give us a push." they replied.

The R.A.F police caught up with us before we could get it on the square!

Cookhouse fatigues were never more than a speck of dust or a dull cap badge away and they were an absolute misery. It's a miracle we weren't traumatised for life by our experiences. Try and imagine a diminutive sixteen year old, stood over a massive sink the size of a small swimming pool, trying to stem a never-ending flow of greasy pots and pans that kept stacking up alongside him. As if this torment wasn't enough, throw in the odd visit from a fickle corporal cook. He'd cast a malevolent glance at your labours and then throw most of the finished pots back in the sink because they weren't clean enough for his liking.

The heat of those kitchens and the sickly, greasy smell of the sink was enough to put you off your food (until tea time anyway!) and your arms, where they were plunged elbow deep in the sink, carried greasy tide marks for ages afterwards.

We lived every second of cookhouse fatigues in an agony of weary drudgery, praying for the end of the day and a lungful of fresh air. The steam from the red hot washing up water would sear your face bright red, whilst sweat rolled under your collar to drive you swearing mad as it trickled maddeningly down your tortured body.

Hell?

Doesn't worry me any more – been there…!

The Devil?

Wouldn't stand a chance against a corporal cook!

Outside the mess was a deep tank of boiling hot water for cleaning our 'irons' in and this, naturally, had its role to play in boy entrant history. What's so side-splittingly hilarious about shoving your mate's hand into boiling water, or throwing his knife and fork into it, I don't know but it seemed really good fun at the time!

It wasn't all doom and gloom though and we coached up to London one pleasant day, to attend the Royal Tournament. It was a good trip and we were suitably impressed with all that went on in the arena, which was a little more impressive than the events that were about to take place outside!

As everyone poured out of one entrance, to make our own way back to the coach, a large contingent of Army boy soldiers exited another entrance and made their way to their coach – directly to our rear. Now, I don't know what's so macho about not politely stepping aside to allow others to pass by without being forced off the pavement, but whatever it is, it affected all of us that night and a major incident almost occurred. Army and R.A.F met head on with shoulders squared, leaving little room for manoeuvre. Collisions took place and bodies were propelled off the pavement with alarming violence as grinning civilians looked on. It was a mute locking of horns though, with little damage done on either side and I'm prepared to accept the result as an honourable draw after all this time – despite the fact that both sides claimed victory on the night!

Fights among us were few and far between but they did occur, sometimes between the best of friends. They were always dealt with in the same way. The fight would be allowed to go on until it became obvious that one had gained an unassailable advantage. The two pro-tagonists would then be separated and told to shake hands.

I never saw anyone refuse to shake hands, even after the fiercest of fights, and I didn't see any friendships suffer afterwards. It was just another robust part of ser-vice life that happened to implant itself on our memories and, hopefully, didn't turn too many of us into rabid hooligans for the rest of our lives!

❖ ❖ ❖

Gymnasium sessions often drew groans of anguish from suffering boy entrants if the disciplines weren't to their liking. Not many of us were keen on the circuit of vaulting horse, balance beam, parallel bars and climbing ropes – they tended to hurt you quite a lot on a fairly regular basis!

"WHAT ARE YOU MOANING ABOUT," a sergeant PTI bellowed at us one day, as we marched into the gym to be confronted with the aforementioned apparatus, "DON'T YOU WANT TO DO PT TODAY?"

No, as a matter of fact, we f***ing well didn't!

Silence.

"WELL, COME ON, LET'S HAVE YOU – ANYONE WHO DOESN'T WANT TO DO PT, FALL OUT AND STAND OVER HERE."

Ginger Troughton fell out and doubled back to the indicated spot. A tense pause and then one or two others went to join him. I don't know why I went, because bravery has never really been my thing but a sort of collected madness affected about twelve of us. We stood in our little, rebellious group and waited for the wrath of God to fall on us.

"OUTSIDE," we were ordered.

Outside the gym was a large tennis court and we were instructed to start running around it.

"DON'T STOP UNTIL YOU'RE ORDERED TO STOP," came our final instruction and we knuckled down to what we guessed would be a very long session. About an hour later, give or take a blister or two, the sergeant PTI came back out to see how things were going.

"HAD ENOUGH? he yelled, "GET BACK INSIDE IF YOU HAVE."

Everybody stayed quiet and kept running. The good sergeant looked thunderous and stormed back indoors. Matters began to deteriorate after that and one or two began to falter as the continued running started to take its toll. One of the lads, whose legs had just about gone, was supported by two of the stronger runners – nobody was to give in on this occasion, no matter what the cost.

Half an hour later, back came the irritable sergeant to stand and stare at us with ill-concealed malice. Sergeant Carl Graffham, one of our trade training instructors, turned up on the scene and heard all about our rebellion from the outraged PTI.

"ALRIGHT, GET BACK INSIDE NOW AND THAT'S AN ORDER YOU BLOODY FOOLS. IT WOULD'VE BEEN A LOT EASIER DOING THE PT WOULDN'T IT?"

Yeah, up yours pal – that's one to us...

Carl Graffham gave us a nod and a secretive grin as we filed past him into the gym.

Sergeant Carl Graffham could give out a good bollocking when required and he considered unruly behaviour in the classroom as good a reason as any to flex his vocal cords. He'd unwisely left us alone to clean the place up one day, omitting to mention that a fairly important gathering of upper echelon personnel was taking place in the building next door. We were in full mayhem mode when he appeared in the doorway like the Angel of death.

"YOU FOOLS – YOU BLOODY FOOLS," he started as we jumped to attention, facing him, "WHEN ARE YOU EVER GOING TO LEARN..." and so on and so forth. This would have been alright in itself, as we could all take a major bollocking with straight-faced solemnity – plenty of practice you see! What we didn't bargain on, was Norm Carver appearing silently to the rear of Sergeant Graffham's left shoulder and starting in on the most amazing set of facial distortions I've ever seen in my life. He accompanied the rolling tirade with a selection of exaggerated frowns, manic grins and a wonderful lop-sided grimace that looked nothing short of maniacal.

We couldn't move and we couldn't avert our eyes. The urge to laugh was overwhelming – the effort to suppress it, suffocating.

Sgt Graffham became aware of Norm's presence and turned to look at him. All he saw was a face that would have shamed a choirboy with its innocence!

We got away with it, but only at the expense of bruised and aching ribs from the pummelling of trapped laughter spasms.

A few sobering thoughts began to creep in as we approached our finals and not just regarding our results. We'd all made good friends during our time at Hereford and it became obvious that we'd soon be splitting up, some for the rest of our service careers. We'd be posted to different stations and it was a lottery as to who would be sent where. The bogey station for suppliers was 16 MU, R.A.F Stafford – Stalag 16, as it was known.

"You don't want to go to bloody Stalag 16," we were told, "it's a nightmare station and it hasn't got any aeroplanes either!"

We all wanted operational stations. If we'd wanted to serve on a station without aeroplanes, we'd have joined the army, wouldn't we? Everyone wanted an overseas tour as quickly as possible but we knew we'd be starting out with a home posting initially and looked forward to trying out man's service for size. Even after eighteen months, the majority of us were still only seventeen, leaving ample time for life's little shocks to maul us about a bit, but we felt we were pretty much invincible at the time – finals permitting, of course!

Life beyond boy's service was hard to imagine. We'd been through eighteen months of rigorous training and were street-wise beyond our years regarding military discipline. We'd taken the knocks and bounced up again without too much damage. It had been fun and it had been rewarding, in equal measures. It didn't occur to us at the time that we'd been through something special together – something that we'd recall with pride many years later, long after the demise of boy entrant service.

The final exams came and went, leaving us in varying states of anticipation.

"I reckon I did alright," ventured one.

"Christ! I'll be lucky if I'm not on Civvy Street next month," came from one doom merchant.

"I just don't know how I got on – what did you put for question five – what! – f**k it, that's one I've definitely got wrong then..."

The long wait for the results was not a happy time and, as we filed into one of the classrooms to learn our fate, the tension was unbearable. At the end of it, I was a very relieved future Senior Aircraftsman. Not everyone passed though and it must have been agonising for the lads that failed. Shamefully, my overwhelming relief at passing far outweighed my sympathy for those who didn't!

The next time we filed into a classroom, it was for our postings.

"Edwards."

"SIR."

"16MU, R.A.F Stafford."

"SIR."

"Stoker."

"SIR."

"16MU, R.A.F Stafford."

"SIR."

"Wetherill."

"SIR."

"16MU, R.A.F Stafford."

"SIR."

"Price."

"SIR."

Look out, here it comes, three to Stalag 16 so far, bound to be something different this time. St Athan's got aeroplanes… or how about Lyneham even. Maybe I'd get posted to…

"16MU, R.A.F Stafford."

"SIR."

Where's Stafford anyway? Anybody know where Stafford is?

Everything was fairly relaxed after our finals but we still had our passing out parade to prepare for and Tommy Temple had set his heart on us making the Coldstream Guards look like ramblers when we marched on to the parade square!

Our parents would be attending on the big day, giving us the opportunity to show off big style – providing we didn't create a shambles on the square. It doesn't take very much at all to throw a parade into embarrassing confusion. A misheard command or losing the step can do it easily and when there are four squadrons linking together, it takes some doing to get it all together.

We didn't intend this to happen.

Parades were never fun events at the best of times and one stood out as a real ordeal. All four squadrons were on the parade square and, for some sadistic reason, we were kept waiting about for a very long time in warm weather. Inevitably, bodies began to teeter and someone from another squadron went down with a clatter.

"Nobody faint – don't go down," somebody from our ranks hissed and Tommy Temple came quietly amongst us with words of advice.

"If you start to feel faint, go up on the balls of your feet. It'll help."

A short while later, I thought I'd give this a try, even though I was okay. No sooner had I raised my heels than Tommy was at my side.

"You alright, son?" he asked quietly.

"Yes, corporal – just practising."

"Well, don't bloody practice in the middle of a parade," he hissed menacingly.

There's just no pleasing some people!

The days leading up to our passing out parade were filled with final preparations for the big day. Best blue uniforms were brushed and pressed until they were immaculate. Boots were bulled all over until they gleamed, webbing belts were whitened and greatcoats were ironed to perfection. Even the black peaks of our caps were buffed to a high shine, whilst every button, cap badge and belt brass gleamed like stars in the sky.

It was a wonderful, euphoric period. No more studying or worrying. No more fretting and fuming over major kit inspections and definitely no more skulking in toilet blocks to avoid church services!

Our day was dawning and we intended to enjoy it to the full. We were going to show off, big style, to our parents and we didn't give a fig for refined dignity and quiet modesty. We were the 43rd and we'd damn well come through eighteen months boy entrant training – we weren't about to succumb to bouts of humility.

We also made peacocks seem shy, when it came to being proud! It would be fair to say that we all left R.A.F Hereford with a massive superiority complex and high expectations.

Friday, 7th December 1962 dawned bright and cold. This was it, our last day of boy entrant training had arrived. We knew parents and family were either on the way or preparing for the journey. Air Vice-Marshal Porter was to be Reviewing Officer and Lofty was going to lead us on as No. 3 Flight Commander. Everybody was immaculate and raring to go, enthusiastic about the coming parade and eager for the leave that was to follow.

We dressed carefully, making sure we didn't scuff our highly bulled boots or mark our white webbing belts and rifle slings. We checked each others kit and adjusted ties until they were straight, then delicately picked our way outside to form up. Tommy Temple checked each and every one of us and gave a nod of satisfaction, along with a few words of encouragement. We formed up for the last time and felt pangs of regret. Everything we did from then on was to be for the last time and it didn't seem possible after eighteen long months of shared comradeship.

The No. 1 Regional Band of the Royal Air Force played us on to the parade square. Four squadrons, providing a colourful display of precision marching. Blue uniforms, white webbing, red and white chequered hatbands - all combined to provide a visual spectacle for watching families and we did them proud. We marched and wheeled, lined up for inspection and finally marched past the Reviewing Officer for the salute. As the squadrons came back along the square, the band struck up with 'Auld Lang Syne' and we went into the slow march. Breaking out into the quick march, we then wheeled off the parade square and out of boy entrant service.

At the billet, Tommy Temple was handing out rail warrants and final instructions, full of smiles and cracks for the benefit of our waiting families. As we went up to him when our names were called, we each tried to find the words to thank him for seeing us through. It generally came out as, "Thanks for everything, Corporal," but I think he understood what we were trying to say. I hope so anyway. It was just as difficult saying goodbye to your mates and we shook hands with a, "See you around, mate," or "Catch up with you sometime."

A lot of us didn't manage that for forty years!

Air Vice-Marshal Porter concluded his address by wishing us all the very best of luck and said, "I hope you will enjoy your time in the service as much as I have enjoyed mine, and I can't wish you any more than that."

None of us made Air Vice-Marshal but I venture to say that we all went on to enjoy our life in the R.A.F immensely and it was the lessons learned in boy's service that carried us through some of the adventures that lay ahead of us on future postings.

❖ ❖ ❖

The eighteen months we went through at Hereford provided us with a rollercoaster ride that took us through high peaks and low troughs at often bewildering speeds – it was a cracking way to start out on the road to manhood.

Rookie: Here Corporal !
I Think The Trigger's Ja........

Epilogue

When I reported to 16MU R.A.F Stafford in 1962, I did so with three others from my entry at Hereford. Ben Stoker, Bob Wetherill and Eddie Edwards. However, we were all posted to different sites and I saw little of them until I applied for the first Air Movements course about a year later. Ben and Bob had applied for the same course and we were re-united at Abingdon for the next two months during the course of our training.

Success with the exams gave us what we so desperately wanted – a posting to a flying station. All three of us were posted to Lyneham in Wiltshire, home of Britannia's, Comet 2s and Comet 4s. We also saw a great variety of freighter aircraft on our job and this was a revelation. Ace Freighters flew Constellations at the time and regularly used to shudder in for a quick turnaround. If we managed it within the hour, the captain always ensured we had a nice donation for the shift beer fund. It also helped if we managed to 'forget' to remove a couple of chains and restraining hooks whilst we were about it (ropes were a poor substitute!).

All three of us would spend our days off pestering the squadrons for a flight and we became quite well known. We'd fly just for the sake of it. Circuits and bumps for hours on end became the norm, then 'down the route' on freight carrying flights to Malta, Aden, Bahrain and

Singapore. During this time, another lad from the 43rd. 'Huck' Bain, our champion diver, joined us.

We parted company a year later when I was posted to the Far East Air Force. Royal Australian Air Force Butterworth to be exact located on the mainland just across from Penang Island. I was just nineteen and still single. It goes without saying that I had the time of my life out there. On one occasion, I was returning from Singapore where I'd been flown for a fencing competition, when a voice boomed out, "Still fencing then, Taff?" It was Bas Tappenden, the very same who'd shouldered some of my burden on Dartmoor. Bas was on a Mobile Air Movements team and we went on to share a posting at R.A.F Western Hill on Penang.

Throughout my service life, I averaged about a year a station. I don't know if it boiled down to the fact that I was invaluable to everyone or that I got up peoples noses! I'd like to think it was the former. On several of these postings, I'd bump into Johnny Davies, a lad who reckoned we saw more of each other post-Hereford than we ever did during our eighteen months training. Whenever I turned up at a new station, I began to expect the familiar shout of, "Hello Taff, what're you doing here?"

I never met up with my own circle of mates from Hereford again, apart from a brief glimpse of Charlie Gibson as I passed through a checkout lounge in Malta. I crossed paths with only two others before I left in 1972. Paul Kinshott was at R.A.F Benson when I arrived and we served together on the Air Movements section. He'd just gone doo-lally over a girl he'd met in a doctor's surgery though and I didn't see much of him after that. They're still happily married. At Thorney Island, I bumped into 'Ginge' Troughton, wearing sergeants stripes and the flying brevet of an Air Quartermaster.

I eventually left the R.A.F in 1972, still single and still wearing the three-bladed propeller denoting my rank of S.A.C. As I started out with a four-bladed propeller I reckon this makes me one of the very few airmen who took a downward turn on the promotion ladder! As I walked through the gates though, I knew that I'd been through a wonderful period in my life and that I'd never enjoy such freedom again.

Everything took a back seat to raising a family after that and I didn't give much thought to joining ex-service organisations until a letter turned up at my mother's address in Wales. The sender was Charlie Gibson, trying to locate me for a planned 40th re-union at Hereford in 2001. I rang him and enjoyed a long chat about old times, during which he asked me if I knew about the Boy Entrants Association. I had to confess ignorance and he duly righted the oversight, persuading me to sign on the dotted line.

Sadly, when the re-union came around, I was unable to attend due to ill health but Charlie made sure I received all the photographs (along with a graphic account of the revelry). It was at this stage, during a prolonged absence from work, that I decided to record our experiences in a book. I sincerely hope that I've done us all justice.

Chris Boxsey, who inadvertently caused me so much grief on the rugby field, called me and talked me into joining BEACHAT, a website for ex-boy entrants. This has proved a very enjoyable experience; with the reminiscences and banter we share often rekindling long lost memories. It isn't difficult at times, to imagine that some of the fun and enthusiasm of fifteen and sixteen year olds is still there in the background.

In 2002, I attended a mini re-union at Hereford with about ten of the lads and their families. It was an incredible experience, if a little disconcerting. The hair was either gone or greying, the faces had a few more lines than they did at fifteen and some of the steps weren't as sprightly as those that marched many a long mile around the parade square at Hereford. The laughter was still intact though and Keithy Brooks, who returned to Hereford as a sergeant instructor, could have stepped straight out of 1961 when telling his tales.

"Boy entrants are no more," I was told when I was carrying out some research at R.A.F Cosford. I was more than happy to enlighten the fresh-faced young gentleman that they most certainly are. Not as sprightly as they once were perhaps but still as proud and cocky as they were when they marched off the parade square on passing out day.

I salute each and every one of them (the RAF way, okay Tommy!)